D0965771

The Wit & Wisdom of
Wall Street

The Wit & Wisdom of
Wall Street

Compiled & Edited by
Bob Thomas

Bascom-Hall Publishing Co.
Dallas, Texas

The Wit & Wisdom of Wall Street
Compiled & Edited by Bob Thomas

Cover Design:
Barton Damer
Email: bartondamer@mac.com
Website: www.alreadybeenchewed.net

Publisher:
Bascom-Hall Publishing Co.
9330 LBJ Freeway
Suite 800
Dallas, Texas 75243
Email: info@bascom-hall.com
Website: www.bascom-hall.com

Additional copies of this book may be ordered from the publisher for $14.95. Please add $3.00 for postage and handling.

Library of Congress Cataloging-in-Publication Data

ISBN-13 978-0-9649201-4-9

Introduction

Wall Street is much more than, as one cynic put it, "a thoroughfare that begins in a graveyard and ends in a river." Rather, Wall Street is the heart of corporate finance in the U.S. and symbolic of investing in the stock market. For many investors, it has proved to be a street paved with gold—while others have truly experienced a "nightmare on Wall Street."

Scores of books and magazine articles have been written over the years detailing how to get rich quick by playing the stock market using a variety of strategies and gimmicks. The truth is, there are no shortcuts and you will not outsmart the market—for very long. But it is very possible to create wealth by investing in the stocks of some of the great companies in America.

Warren Buffett, one of the richest men in the world, accumulated his tremendous wealth by being a savvy and patient investor in the stock market. In fact, he once described his investment philosophy as "lethargy bordering on sloth."

The Wit & Wisdom of Wall Street includes quotes from leading investment gurus such as Benjamin Graham, Warren Buffett, Peter Lynch, John Templeton, Jason Zweig, and many others, along with axioms, one-liners, and clever cartoons from the esteemed *New Yorker* magazine; all about investing on Wall Street. Hopefully, you will be entertained and amused by the wit—but more importantly, you should become wealthier and wiser from the wisdom.

Bob Thomas

"The stock market is like a beauty contest; you shouldn't necessarily pick the prettiest girl—pick the one everyone else thinks is the prettiest."

– John Maynard Keynes

"Be greedy when others
are fearful—and fearful
when others are greedy."

– Warren Buffett

Every time someone buys,
someone sells—and both
think they're brilliant.

By ignoring the losers and
taking profits in the winners—
you eventually end up with
a portfolio of losers.

The stock market depends about as much on stock market analysts as the weather does on weather forecasters.

Fundamental analysis will tell you what stocks to buy—technical analysis will tell you when to buy them.

"If you're compulsively
checking up on the prices
of your investments, you're
not only hurting your financial
returns, you're unnecessarily
taking precious time away
from the rest of your life."

– *Jason Zweig*

"The least risky long-term style of buying stocks is to buy the stocks that refuse to go down on bad news."

– *Justin Mamis*

"The one single thought that sustains me is that the fundamentals are good."

75% of the risk in any stock is the
market and the sector.

Having live streaming quotes on your
computer is like having a slot machine
on your desk.

Take your money seriously. You shouldn't
have fun investing—that's a trap;
it makes you too active.

A bull must be fed every day with good news—but a bear needs only to be fed once in a while.

Many times a buy-and-hold investment is a short-term trade that went wrong.

A market decline should be viewed as an opportunity to buy high quality stocks—not a disaster.

The longer a stock trades in a very narrow range, the more explosive it will move when it ultimately breaks out—in either direction.

"Bull markets are
born in pessimism,
grow in skepticism,
mature in optimism,
and die in euphoria."

– John Templeton

"The chief losses to investors come from the purchase of low-quality securities at times of favorable conditions."

– *Benjamin Graham*

When bad news can't take the
market down—it's good news.

Never buy a stock that didn't
rise in a bull market—smart
investors are out of it.

If it looks too good to be true
you haven't read the
prospectus carefully enough.

Good investment advice is
expensive—bad investment
advice is very expensive.

When the covers of major
business magazines feature
an investment trend in a bearish
light it is very likely that the
trend is at or near its bottom.

"Be that way, Marilyn. You weren't sneering at me when I was managing your portfolio."

"The key to making money in stocks
is not to get scared out of them."

– Peter Lynch

"It's wise to remember that too
much success in the stock market
is in itself an excellent warning."

– Gerald Loeb

Never confuse brilliance on your part with a bull market.

Most portfolios do worse than the averages over the long term.

Why is it that if you can buy all you want of an IPO, you don't want any—and if you can't obtain any, you want to buy all you can get?

"Markets can remain irrational longer than you can remain solvent."

– John Maynard Keynes

"Investors turning to technical analysis is roughly analogous to consulting a fortune teller."

– Laszlo Birinyi Jr.

"For those properly prepared in advance, a bear market in stocks is not a calamity—it's an opportunity."

– John Templeton

"When hamburgers go down in price, we sing the 'Hallelujah Chorus' in the Buffett household; when hamburgers go up, we weep. For most people it's the same way with everything in life—except stocks."

– *Warren Buffett*

"What actually registers in the stock market's fluctuations are not the events themselves—but the human reactions to those events."

– Bernard Baruch

"Get inside information from the President and you'll probably lose half of your money—get it from the Chairman of the Board and you'll lose all of it."

– Jim Rogers

When in doubt—sell.

Always buy and sell
at the market.

Don't hold losers—swap
bad stocks for good ones.

Never buy a stock just after a
significant rise or sell one just
after a significant drop.

An extraordinarily high dividend
rate may indicate an eventual
dividend cut.

Don't buy the sympathy stock—buy
the stock of the company that is
actually moving higher.

"Thousands of experts study overbought indicators, oversold indicators, head-and-shoulders patterns, put-call ratios, the Fed's policy on money supply, foreign investment, the movement of the constellations through the heavens, and the moss on oak trees—and they can't predict markets with any useful consistency any more than the gizzard squeezers could tell the Roman emperors when the Huns would attack."

– *Peter Lynch*

Bad days in the market precede rallies more often than declines.

If an abnormal return is promised— there must be an abnormal risk.

Don't be fooled by these four deadly words—"It's different this time."

"Up a hundred and sixteen points! If only we'd
had the foresight to invest ten minutes ago."

"The worst mistake investors make is taking their profits too soon and their losses too long."

– Michael Price

"A diminishing number of new highs, as the DJIA keeps chugging higher, warns of a forthcoming top."

– Justin Mamis

"Start investing now, not later. Don't worry about whether the market is high or low— just begin investing. Trust in time rather than timing."

– *Burton Malkiel*

"The public is right during the trends—but wrong at both ends."

– Humphrey Neill

"Investors repeatedly jump ship on a good strategy just because it hasn't worked so well lately— and almost invariably abandon it at precisely the wrong time."

– David Dreman

There are more advances in a
bear market than there are
declines in a bull market.

Resist the temptation to invest
in new issues—most will
ultimately be losers.

The best defense in the face
of an impending correction
is owning great stocks.

No one was ever ruined
taking a profit.

Don't be a bull or a bear
all of the time.

When three or more insiders
are buying—follow them.

"Wall Street has a uniquely hysterical way of thinking the world will end tomorrow but be fully recovered in the long run—then a few years later believing the immediate future is rosy but that the long term stinks."

– Kenneth Fisher

Bull markets typically last
longer than bear markets.

Never sell half of a position—
sell it all and walk away.

A market falling on light volume
tends to rise fairly soon.

"The only value of stock market forecasters is to make fortune tellers look good."

– Warren Buffett

When you get an unreasonably
quick profit take it and pay the taxes.

The out-of-favor stock of a
good company will eventually
come back strong.

The more stocks go up, the more
people think stocks can go up—
but that can't go on forever.

"I see you've managed to hold on
to yesterday's gains."

Selling right is half solved by
buying right.

Never check stock prices on
Friday—it could spoil
your weekend.

If Santa Claus should fail to call—
bears may come to Broad
and Wall.

"There has been a remarkable uniformity in the conclusions of studies done on all forms of technical analysis—but not one has consistently out-performed the placebo of a buy-and-hold strategy."

– *Burton Malkiel*

"Bears supply the balance wheel to haphazard speculation."

– Bernard Baruch

"You don't want analysts in a bear market—and you don't need them in a bull market."

– Gerald Loeb

On Wall Street, optimism sells better
than pessimism.

If your investments are keeping you
awake at night—sell down to
the sleeping point.

In a correction, the market goes down
much faster than it goes up as panicked
investors stampede to get out.

Never hold on to a loser just to collect the dividends.

Buy-and-hold investors should strongly consider stocks with rising dividends.

Companies repurchasing their stock in the market typically has a positive effect on share price.

"Any man who is a bear on the future of this country will go broke."

– J.P. Morgan

"There are two times in a man's life when he should not speculate—when he can't afford it, and when he can."

– Mark Twain

"Trying to time the market is not likely to add value to your investments—it is likely to be counter-productive."

– John Bogle

"If you buy a diversified portfolio of low P/E, low cash-flow, or low price-to-book stocks you'll outperform the market pretty significantly."

– David Dreman

"I don't buy stocks simply because others are
buying them. I buy them because many, many
others are buying them."

Buying a stock trading above its 200 day moving average tends to have positive results.

When holding a good stock with an excessive price—wait for the earnings to catch up.

Never buy a stock that won't go up in a bull market—never sell a stock that won't go down in a bear market.

"The unwillingness of investors and commentators to accept a bull market bodes well for the market."

– *Laszlo Birinyi Jr.*

"Far more money has been lost by investors preparing for corrections, or trying to anticipate corrections, than has been lost in corrections themselves."

– *Peter Lynch*

"The average long-term experience
in investing is never surprising—
but the short-term experience
is always surprising."

– Charles Ellis

"If diversification was successful
why would so many money managers
so consistently underperform the
averages year after year, and most
glaringly, in bearish years?"

– Justin Mamis

Never make a decision to
sell on Sunday morning.

Nobody rings a bell when
a bull market is over.

High yields attract investors—
outrageously high yields attract fools.

If you're depending on hope
and prayer—it's time to get out.

Don't be afraid to sell a winner—
pay yourself for being smart.

At most brokerage firms the
word *sell* is spelled *h-o-l-d*.

"I tend to be more conservative as markets go up—and more aggressive as markets go down."

– *Charles Royce*

You can't control the market but you can control your reaction to it.

Don't be deluded, a loss is a loss—whether on paper or actual.

You might be right about where the market is going—but you have no idea where it will go after that.

"There will always be bull markets followed by bear markets, followed by bull markets."

– John Templeton

"The worse a situation becomes, the less it takes to turn it around— and the bigger the upside."

– George Soros

"Charts not only tell what was, they tell what is; and a trend from *was* to *is* contains better percentages than clumsy guessing."

– *Robert. A. Levy*

"I know you didn't tell me to sell, Arthur, but when I said 'Maybe this is the time to sell,' you paused."

"The hard-to-accept great paradox in the stock market is that what seems too high and risky to the majority usually goes higher—and what seems too low and cheap usually goes lower."

– *William O'Neil*

Human nature is always in conflict
with successful investing.

Never sell a stock that has long
been inactive just at the moment
it begins to move ahead.

When the shorter-term of two moving
averages crosses above the longer-
term moving average it's a buy signal.

Take windfall profits when
you have them.

A classic bull market starts with
a run-up in the prices of
blue chip stocks.

Ever notice that investors love to
talk about their stocks going up—but
not a peep when they're going down.

"My biggest winners continue
to be stocks I've held for three
and even four years."

– Peter Lynch

"The intelligent investor is likely
to need considerable will power
to keep from following the crowd."

– Benjamin Graham

"It's a loser's game to pay a premium for stocks based on somebody's estimate of what the company will do the year after next or even the next quarter."

– *David Dreman*

If you put all your eggs in one basket—watch that basket!

It's always a bull market in the long run—if not, no one would buy stocks.

The new high list will do better in the subsequent six months than the new low list.

"Only buy something that you'd be perfectly happy to hold if the market shut down for 10 years."

– Warren Buffett

"Never pay the slightest attention to what a company president ever says about his stock."

– Bernard Baruch

There's more anxiety
in being *out* of a bull
market than being
in a bear market.

"If the business does well the stock eventually follows."

– Warren Buffett

"A falling stock market is the necessary first step to buying low."

– Charles Ellis

"I told you the Fed should have tightened."

"Don't wait until the time or market is just right to start investing—start now. The best time to plant an oak tree was 20 years ago— the second best time is now."

– James Stowers

A stock that goes down 50% and comes back 50% is still down 25%.

Trading isn't a game of luck—it's a game of probability.

Trying to time the purchase of a dropping stock is like trying to catch a falling knife.

A watched stock never boils.

More stocks double than go to zero.

A bull market climbs a wall of worry.

"You can think more objectively with cash in your account than you can if you are worrying about a stock that has lost money for you. There are other securities where your chance of recouping your loss could be far greater."

– *William O'Neil*

"It does little good to purchase the right stocks if the next time the market trembles you find yourself scurrying to the safety of money market assets."

– *Jeremy Siegel*

Watch the company—not the stock price.

Stock gains are determined by the growth of earnings and dividends.

Bailing out of a good stock with the idea of jumping back in later is how most investors get burned.

"In the book of things people more often do wrong than right, investing must certainly top the list—followed closely by wallpapering and eating artichokes."

– *Robert Klein*

"Oh, I'm really sorry. I just placed three million with some broker who called five minutes ago."

Don't hold on to a mistake.

Markets usually anticipate.

A stock does not know you own it.

"Buy high, sell higher."

– William O'Neil

"Forget about trying to time the market—let compounding go to work for you."

– David Dreman

"Averaging down in a bear market
is tantamount to taking a seat
on the down escalator at Macy's."

– Richard Russell

"There are few if any chronic
bears as pessimists have a hard
time making a living in America."

– John Rothchild

"I guarantee that the stock market will be a lot higher in 15 years, and even higher in 25—but I don't know where it will be Monday."

– *Peter Lynch*

"Unless you can watch your stock holdings decline by 50% without becoming panic stricken, you should not be in the stock market."

– *Warren Buffett*

Buy the dips—sell the rallies.

Market trends are not constructed
by previous highs or lows.

Nothing is more dangerous in
a falling market than a calm
reaction to the decline.

"Investors may be quite willing to take the risk of being wrong in the company of others—while being much more reluctant to take the risk of being right alone."

– *John Maynard Keynes*

"Just when I realize I'm beginning to lose faith in the economy, the market hits another all time high."

Doing nothing while a substantial profit disappears just to avoid paying taxes is folly.

The first time a company reduces its earnings estimate is bad—the second time is usually disastrous.

"I found dollar-cost averaging to be a successful over-all strategy as long as one concentrated on stock purchases of companies that demonstrated consistent earnings and dividend growth. Dollar-cost averaging can be disastrous if you fail to purchase stocks that are continually increasing in value."

– *George Connell*

Long-term investors should want
to see stocks lower.

Time is the friend of stocks—the
enemy of bonds.

Your emotions are often a reverse
indicator of what you ought to be doing.

"Down cycles are not fun—
you never know whether this
one is a down cycle or the
beginning of the end."

– Robert Rubin

January tends to set the tone for the rest of the year.

News on stocks is not important—how the stock reacts to it is important.

Stocks always seem to rise on the day before a holiday—any holiday.

"Why is it that it takes a real bear market to get analysts interested in the value approach?"

– Benjamin Graham

"There are a thousand stocks out there that could make you rich, totally independent of what you do for a living."

– Jim Cramer

"Spend at least as much time researching a stock as you would choosing a refrigerator."

– Peter Lynch

"Analysts blamed the market's volatility on computer-directed trading while computers blamed it on analyst-directed trading."

Markets always go to extremes.

Markets are never wrong—personal
opinions are often wrong.

When selecting a stock to buy,
select the one you think you
will never have a reason to sell.

"All bull markets undergo sharp drops along their way to a peak. Such periodic washouts are common and are necessary for a mega-market to be sustainable over the long run."

– *Ralph Acampora*

A company's first earnings
disappointment won't be the last.

Cyclical stocks tend to lead the
market in economic recoveries.

Low inflation and low interest rates
usually result in a strong stock market.

"Never, ever, ever, under any circumstance, add to a losing position—not ever, not never! Adding to losing positions is trading's carcinogen; it is trading's driving while intoxicated. It will lead to ruin. Count on it!"

– *Dennis Gartman*

"Don't try to buy at the bottom and sell at the top. This can't be done—except by liars."

– *Bernard Baruch*

"If the job has been correctly done when a common stock is purchased, the time to sell it is almost never."

– *Philip Fisher*

As a bull market begins to peak, sell the stock that has gone up the most—it will drop the fastest. Also sell the stock that has gone up the least—it didn't go up, so it has to go down.

Don't buck the trend—your trade won't be the one that turns the market around.

Be critical when reading an annual report and pay special attention to the footnotes.

"Careful pal, you're talking about the stocks I love."

Don't be loyal to your stocks—
save that for your football team.

Fear and greed are stronger
than long-term resolve.

When all the experts and
forecasts agree—something
else is going to happen.

"Value stocks are about as exciting as watching grass grow—but have you ever noticed just how much your grass grows in a week?"

– *Christopher Browne*

High risk seldom equals high return.

If the idea is right, eighths and
quarters won't matter.

When investing for 10 years or longer,
there isn't much difference between
load and no-load mutual funds.

"A pack of lemmings looks like
a group of rugged individualists
compared with Wall Street when
it gets a concept in its teeth."

– Warren Buffett

"Markets invariably move to undervalued and overvalued extremes because human nature falls victim to greed and fear."

– William Gross

"There's no reason why stocks that are up a lot should drop—just as there's no reason why stocks that have cratered have to come back eventually."

– Pat Dorsey

Don't be too concerned
about overpaying by a little
when buying a good stock—
over a five- or ten-year holding
period it will be meaningless.

To create long-term wealth—be an investor, not a speculator.

A bubble is a bull market in which you don't have a position.

Every stock investor should have 10% of their portfolio in gold—and hope it doesn't go up in value.

"Harold, have you reaped huge gains that
you have not told me about?"

A bull market is like sex—when it feels best, it's almost over.

Whenever you invest in a sure thing—hedge.

The more confused the investor, the more absolute certainty he will demand from his financial advisor.

"Sell for a reason, not just because the stock did well for one year—never jump off a moving train."

– *Peter Lynch*

"If you take the time to choose only the stocks of great companies, you will still be hurt when the market pulls back. But you will be able to sleep easy in the knowledge that your stocks will lead the next bull charge up the mountain."

– *Stephen Leeb*

Buy when there's blood in
the streets.

Average up, not down—add to
winners, not losers.

The market's daily open belongs
to the amateurs—the close
belongs to the professionals.

Volume is validity.

When they tell you not
to panic—run!

Bear markets begin in good
times—bull markets begin
in bad times.

"Benign neglect is, for most investors, the secret to long-term success in investing."

– Charles Ellis

Take profits relentlessly.

Never let a winner turn into a loser.

Wall Street is motivated primarily by
two emotions—fear and greed.

"Has there been any unusual activity in
our stock? The canary just died."

"Rallies in bear markets die
on low volume."

– Art Cashin

"The faster a stock has run up
in value—the faster it is likely
to run down."

– Robert Menschel

"If owning stocks is a long-term project for you, following their changes constantly is a very, very bad idea. It's the worst possible thing you can do, because people are so sensitive to short-term losses."

– *Daniel Kahneman*

Long shots rarely pay off.

Sell your worst performing
stock first.

There will be a bear market—
there always is.

"The time to buy securities is when the media is so full of doom and gloom that your trembling hand can barely hold the telephone to call your broker with a buy order."

– *James Michaels*

"Don't gamble; take all your savings and buy a good stock, and hold it till it goes up, then sell it. If it don't go up—don't buy it."

– *Will Rogers*

The magic of compound interest.

If you received $1,000 a day for 30 days you would end up with $30,000. If, on the other hand, you received one penny the first day, then double the previous day's total the second day and so on for the entire 30 days, you would end up with an astonishing $10,737,418.23. Halfway into the 30 days you would only have $327.67, but does it ever pick up steam over the second half.

Moral: Reinvest all dividends, interest, and capital gains distributions.

"No matter what the mistake was, it's rarely worth hanging on to a stock that you bought for a reason that is no longer valid. Cut your losses and move on."

– *Pat Dorsey*

"I know I said I would marry you, but that was four hundred points ago!"

Better to pay a fair price for a good company than a cheap price for a loser.

CDs, treasury bills, and money market funds are not investments—just places to park your money while you decide where to invest.

"With enough inside information and a million dollars, you can go broke in a year."

– Warren Buffett

Buy right—hold tight.

Markets must reverse.

In a bull market, be bullish.

"Everyone has the brain power to make money in stocks—not everyone has the stomach. If you are susceptible to selling everything in a panic, you ought to avoid stocks and mutual funds altogether."

– *Peter Lynch*

Turn around situations rarely turn.

Only speculate with what you can afford to lose.

A stock must stay above its moving average for the up-trend to be considered valid and in force.

"The market is like a train sitting on the tracks. You can see the direction it's heading but you cannot dictate the time of departure. Those investors who put the market on a timetable not only become frustrated but end up making foolish moves. Instead, get on the train, sit back, and enjoy the scenery."

– *Roger Engemann*

"Rallies that follow good news are not nearly as likely to last as those that anticipate the event."

– *Laszlo Birinyi Jr.*

"I won't be able to handle your account anymore as it suddenly appears that you're a small investor."

©Leo Cullum/ The New Yorker Collection/www.cartoonbank.com

"The crowd is most enthusiastic and optimistic when it should be cautious and prudent—and is most fearful when it should be bold."

– Humphrey Neill

Avoid fad industries.

Patience neutralizes risk.

Wall Street hates surprises.

No price is too high for a bull or too low for a bear.

Be bullish on stocks that out-perform the market.

Large cap stocks tend to do better in a bear market than small cap stocks.

"There's no shame in losing money on a stock—everybody does it. What is shameful is to hold on to a stock, or, worse, to buy more of it, when the fundamentals are deteriorating."

– *Peter Lynch*

"Bears don't live on Park Avenue."

– Bernard Baruch

"The only way to make money buying overpriced stocks is if they become even more overpriced."

– Michael Metz

To be a successful market timer,
you would have to be right twice;
when you buy and when you sell. To
be right the first time, you have a 50%
chance—to be right on both sides of
the trade you have a 25% chance.

"A bull market is illogical, irrational, and you can't diagnose how far it is going to go—but it always ends. Then you have a bear market, and during that you can usually tell the bottom."

– *Roy Neuberger*

"I'd love to ask you in, Howard, but they start trading in Hong Kong in ten minutes."

You can't make money
breaking even.

Price is what you pay—
value is what you get.

Most stocks fluctuate 50%
from low to high each year.

"Buy to the sound of cannons, sell to the sound of trumpets."

– Lord Nathan Rothschild

The easiest way to go broke is
being right too soon.

When market optimism is really frothy,
stocks seem to be discounting not
only the future but even the hereafter.

"In this game, the market has to keep pitching, but you don't have to swing. You can stand there with the bat on your shoulder for six months until you get a fat pitch."

– Warren Buffett

"The modern financial history of the U.S. holds no example of a physical disaster, or even an outright war, that wreaked lasting havoc on investment returns."

– Jason Zweig

How the market reacts to bad news is more important than the news itself.

Why buy stock of laggard companies hoping for a turn-around, when there are plenty of stocks already heading in the right direction.

Stock splits generally bode well
for investors.

The market never discounts the
same thing twice.

The pain of losing is greater than
the pleasure of winning.

"On Wall Street today, the stock market corrected
its previous correction, and is pretty sure
it's got it right this time."

A rising tide lifts all boats.

Never buy just to get a dividend.

Buy stocks when the market is depressed.

"I don't know what the seven wonders of the world are, but I do know the eighth—compound interest."

– Baron Rothschild

"Look at a stock as a business, instead of a piece of paper that moves up and down."

– William Ruane

"A small loss, when realized, becomes an opportunity for profit elsewhere. It gives you the chance to turn a liability into an asset, instead of just sitting there praying that your old stock will come back."

– Martin Zweig

The biggest mistake you can make in
a powerful bull market is to sell
good stocks too early.

It's best to wait until a market collapse
actually starts—when it's too high, it
can still go much higher.

Bull markets have no resistance—
bear markets have no support.

The bottom is almost always 10%
below your worst case expectation.

Don't panic if your stock has a sharp
downturn for days or weeks—it can and
has happened to even great stocks.

"Timidity prompted by past failures causes investors to miss the most important bull markets."

– Walter Schloss

Every stock investor should have 10% of their portfolio in gold—and hope it doesn't go up in value.

A company's earnings estimates tend to impact its stock more dramatically than actual earnings results.

Stocks with low cash flow multiples typically outperform those with high multiples by more than 4-to-1.

"The market hit new highs today, while the contrition index remained at zero."

"For most people, the decision to sell depends more on what a stock has done than on what it is likely to do."

– Terrance Odean

"Buy when the market is making new tops and higher bottoms—sell when the market is making lower tops and lower bottoms."

– W. D. Gann

Avoid the roller coaster of worry by not checking your stock prices every day. How often do you check on the value of your home?

By selling stocks to avoid pain—
you can miss the next gain.

Historically, stocks only increase
11% a year on average.

There is less risk in selling short
in a bear market than buying
in a bull market.

"Nobody can predict interest rates, the future direction of the economy, or the stock market. Dismiss all such forecasts and concentrate on what's actually happening to the companies in which you've invested."

– *Peter Lynch*

"An investment strategy is not worth much if you constantly change due to a lack of underlying confidence or comfort. This is the difference between investing and playing the market."

– *Peter Skirkanich*

Companies growing at greater than
50% per year cannot keep it up.

As an investor, don't permit yourself
to be sidetracked by negative rumors
or the possibility of quick profits
from a speculation.

"If you expect to continue to purchase stocks throughout your life, you should welcome price declines as a way to add stocks more cheaply to your portfolio."

– Warren Buffett

"Trading is heavy today."

Best tip the market will ever give you—never answer a margin call.

Big drops in the market are almost always great buying opportunities.

When the stock market makes the front page of the newspapers and everybody is talking stocks—the bull market is just about over.

"Lower trading volume, while
the price continues to advance,
is an unsustainable condition
and warns of a reversal."

– Don Cassidy

All booms go bust.

Volume precedes price.

Winners keep on winning.

"One of the best rules anybody can learn about investing is to do nothing, absolutely nothing, unless there is something to do. Most people always have to be playing—they always have to be doing something."

– *Jim Rogers*

When it's time to buy—you
won't want to.

Don't panic when the market
seems to be falling apart.

In a high market confine yourself
to high-quality stocks.

"Bear market corrections
are more violent and
far swifter than bull
market corrections."

– Dennis Gartman

"The riskiest moment is when you're right. That's when you're in the most trouble, because you tend to over-stay the good decisions."

– *Peter Bernstein*

"Hey, investor fears need calming over here, too."

"I have almost infinite patience for a stock that's going down if the business is growing well."

– *William Nygren*

"When unemployment is rising, buy stocks—when unemployment is falling, avoid stocks."

– Stephen Leeb

"A prospectus is not designed to help investors—it is designed to disclose legal requirements."

– Michael Lipper

"Money is made by discounting the
obvious and betting on
the unexpected."

– George Soros

"In investing money, the amount
of investment you want should
depend on whether you want
to eat well or sleep well."

– J. Kenfield Morley

Successful investors have the courage to buy while others are selling, and the courage to sell when others are buying.

Don't be afraid to buy a stock making new highs. A stock at a new high of 50 must keep making new highs at 55, 57, and 59 on the way to 60.

"A loss never bothers me after
I take it; I forget it. But being
wrong, not taking the loss—that
is what does damage to the
pocketbook and to the soul."

– Jesse Livermore

There is a time to buy, a time to sell—
and a long time to do nothing.

Stocks are never too high to begin
buying—or too low to begin selling.

Don't buy a stock just because
it has an abnormally low P/E—it's
probably low for a reason.

"The people who are buying stocks because they're going up and don't know what they do, deserve to lose money."

– *Jim Cramer*

"Prices have no memory, and yesterday has nothing to do with tomorrow. Every day starts out 50-50—yesterday's price discounted everything yesterday."

– *Adam Smith*

"I want each of you on the way home tonight to stop, look up, ponder the heavens, and consider how insignificant our second-quarter really is."

Before selling—wait for the worry to actually happen.

In a bear market, big stocks do better than small ones.

The market tends to have a sell-off every fall.

"People who exit the stock market
to avoid a decline are odds-on
favorites to miss the next rally."

– Peter Lynch

"If a battered stock refuses to sink any
lower no matter how many negative
articles appear in the papers—
that stock is worth a close look."

– James L. Fraser

When institutions and mutual funds decide they made a mistake and they want out, there isn't a door wide enough for all of them to get out.

When in doubt—stay out.

Swing for singles—not home runs.

It's easier to stay out than to get out.

At market bottoms almost
everything is ridiculously
cheap—at the tops everything
is extravagantly overpriced.

"The stock market always seems to find news appropriate to its frame of mind."

– Albert Haas Jr.

"Lethargy bordering on sloth remains the cornerstone of my investment style."

– Warren Buffett

Investigate—then invest.

The market hates uncertainty.

Buy carefully—sell reluctantly.

"If we're being honest, it was your decision to follow
my recommendations that cost you money."

Even if you invest when the market is going up, you may not be in the right stocks—the Dow rose 25% in 1999 but 60% of the stocks on the NYSE did not increase.

"To win at investing you have to
be in the minority."

– John Maynard Keynes

"It was never my thinking that made
me money—it was my sitting."

– Jesse Livermore

"The first stocks to double in a bull
market will usually double again."

– Michael Burke

"The serious investor knows that among the many signposts that point to corporate and investment growth, a rising dividend trend is perhaps the most significant."

– *Geraldine Weiss*

Almost nobody has the courage to get off the bandwagon of highly over-priced stocks when it's in full gear.

The odds are greater that the market will continue in the same direction it is going—than that it will reverse direction.

Buy when doom and gloom
is everywhere.

Bottoms take longer to form and
tend to be smaller than tops.

Even though you're familiar with
a stock, you should be as willing
to reject it as to accept it.

"More people get killed chasing
after a higher yield than looking
down the barrel of a gun."

– William LeFevre

"Profits tend to be substantially
lower and life pretty much more
stressful when buying and selling
stocks for short-term profits."

– Philip Fisher